Sikhs
Legacy of the Punjab

Fig. 1. North entrance to the exhibition *Sikhs: Legacy of the Punjab* at the Smithsonian's National Museum of Natural History, Washington, D.C. (2004)

The exhibition *Sikhs: Legacy of the Punjab* was initially produced by the National Museum of Natural History, Smithsonian Institution. The curatorial team (Asian Cultural History Program, Department of Anthropology) included curator Paul Michael Taylor, with the help of Michel D. Lee, Randy S. Tims, Kyle A. Lemargie, Christopher Lotis, and others; Vijay S. Chattha helped coordinate associated events. In 2006-2007, Robert Pontsioen served as guest curator of the added components on Punjabi music. Researchers Jared Koller, Trevor Merrion, and Jasper Waugh-Quasebarth assisted with documentation and photography of newly added artworks at the Fresno venue. Other creative exhibition content for the original Smithsonian exhibition was provided by designer Tom Thill, script writer/editor Sarah Grusin, and educational outreach coordinator Junko Chinen. Michael Mason, Cindy Blekas, Rena Selim, and others provided administrative and production support within the Department of Exhibits. Hanna Szczepanowska served as exhibition conservator; Prof. Gurinder S. Mann (University of California, Santa Barbara) served as the Smithsonian's external reviewer of the exhibition content. For organizational efforts and support at subsequent venues, special thanks are due to former director Karl Hutterer at the Santa Barbara Museum of Natural History, and to director Linda Cano at the Fresno Art Museum, and to the exhibition and curatorial staff of both museums.

The authors of this book sincerely thank the peer reviewers for their comments. The design and printing of this book have been made possible by generous contributions from the **Sikh Heritage Foundation** (Weirton, West Virginia) and from:

Gurpreet Singh Ahuja & Jasjit Kaur Ahuja
Association of Sikh Professionals
Bhasin Family
Jaswinder K. Chattha & Amrik S. Chattha
Sohan S. Chaudhary & Kamal K. Chaudhary
Khurana Family
Bhupinder S. Mac & Amarjit K. Mac
Surendrapal Singh Mac & Harjit B Mac
Malik Family of Delhi
Malik Family of Los Angeles
Jagtar Singh Sandhu
Sawhney Family
Sikh Arts & Film Festival (www.sikhlens.com)
Sikh Spirit Foundation
Harvinder Singh & Paramjeet Kaur
Manbir Singh & Taran Kaur

The production and Smithsonian installation of *Sikhs: Legacy of the Punjab* was made possible through the generosity of the following donors:

Drs. Amrik S. and Jaswinder K. Chattha
Grewal Family and Singh Development, LLC
in memory of Sardar Sarwan Singh Grewal
Ms. Rajinder Kaur Keith, in memory of Ms. Narinder K. Keith

Dr. & Mrs. Sohan S. and Kamaljit K. Chaudhary
Dr. & Mrs. Brijinder S. and Manorma K. Kochhar
Mr. & Mrs. Gurdip S. and Nirmaljeet K. Malik
Dr. & Mrs. Charn S. and Surinder K. Nandra
Drs. Harvinder S. and Asha K. Sahota
Drs. Harvinder S. and Sonia K. Sandhu
Prehlad S. Vachher, M.D.

And through the generosity of:
Dr. & Mrs. Ajit S. and Rita K. Arora
Mr. & Mrs. Kuldip S. and Pinderpal K. Bains
Dr. & Mrs. Kamaljit S. and Kavelle K. Bajaj
Drs. Surinder S. and Jagdeep K. Bajwa
Mrs. Manjeet K. Bansal and grandchildren
Mr. & Mrs. Balbir S. and Kuldeep K. Basi
Dr. & Mrs. Guriqbal S. and Jagdish K. Basi, and Amar Iqbal and Heera Basi
Dr. & Mrs. Raghbir S. and Brijinder K. Basi and Rajpreet S. Basi
Dr. Manraj S. Bath
Drs. Samir M. and Amita K. Bhatt
Sardar & Sardarni Ishar S. and Kuljit K. Bindra
Dr. & Mrs. Balbir S. and Raminder K. Brar
Drs. Rakesh and Joceliza Chaudhary
Drs. Satpal S. and Komal Kiron K. Dang
Mr. & Mrs. Mohinder S. and Pawan K. Datta
Dr. & Mrs. Prabhjot S. and Sheena Deol
Drs. Eldan B. and Geetinder K. Chattha Eichbaum
Dr. & Mrs. Narinder S. and Jasbir K. Gahunia
Sardar & Sardarni Jagir S. and Bachan K. Grewal
Drs. Sachinder S. and Bijaya A. Hans
Mr. & Mrs. Daljit S. and Rajinder K. Khara
Drs. Surendrapal S. and Harjit Bala Mac
Dr. & Mrs. Baljeet S. and Reena K. Mahal
Dr. & Mrs. Jasbir S. and Vickie C. Makar
Drs. Jasbir S. and Satinder K. Mann
Dr. & Mrs. Sarabjit S. and Jaspal K. Neelam
in memory of Paboji Gurdev Kaur Neelam
Dr. & Mrs. Nirmal S. and Balbir K. Nilvi
Dr. & Mrs. Gurnam S. and Khushwant K. Pannu
Dr. & Mrs. Sardul S. and Surinderjit G. Pannu
Dr. & Mrs. Tarlok S. and Amarjit K. Purewal
Mr. & Mrs. Ajit S. and Kanwaljit K. Randhava
Mr. & Mrs. Harbhajan S. and Sharanjit K. Samra
Drs. Rajbir S. and Satwant K. Samra
Mr. & Mrs. Sukhminder S. and Ranjit K. Sandhu
Drs. & Mrs. Ujjal S. and Sukhbinder K. Sandhu
Drs. Jagjit S. and Parkash K. Sehdeva, and Pauljeet S. Sehdeva
Drs. Baljit S. and Jatinder K. Sidhu
Sikh Heritage Foundation (Weirton, West Virginia)
Drs. Navtej S. and Rekha K. Singh
Drs. Piara S. and Kamla K. Singh
Dr. & Mrs. Ranjeet S. and Justine Overturf Singh
Mr. & Mrs. Ajit S. and Darshan K. Thiara

And many other donors and supporters of the Smithsonian's Sikh Heritage Project.

Fig. 2. Detail of Ceremonial Sikh Helmet
Gilded copper, 13.5 x 18 x 23.1
c. 1805-1840
Courtesy of the Kapany Collection of Sikh Art

Fig. 3. *Nishān*
Steel
21st century
Courtesy of the Sikh Heritage Foundation

Fig. 4. Entrance leading to the Darbar Sahib, Amritsar, Punjab, India. (2006)

Fig. 5. Darbar Sahib, Amritsar, Punjab, India. (2006)

Sikhs
Legacy of the Punjab

Paul Michael Taylor | Robert Pontsioen

Asian Cultural History Program
Smithsonian Institution

In association with:

Sikh Heritage Foundation
(Weirton, West Virginia)

Fresno Art Museum
(Fresno, California)

The Sikh Foundation
(Palo Alto, California)

This book is produced and distributed by: Asian Cultural History Program, Department of Anthropology, Smithsonian Institution, Washington D.C. 20560 USA. In association with: Sikh Heritage Foundation (Weirton, West Virginia), Fresno Art Museum (Fresno, California), and The Sikh Foundation (Palo Alto, California).

ISBN: 978-1-891739-90-3
First edition. First printing.

Design by KI Graphics (Springfield, Virginia, USA). Printed in India by Aravali Printers.
ISBN 978-1-891739-90-3 (hardcover)
First edition. First printing.

Published in conjunction with the exhibition *Sikhs: Legacy of the Punjab*, organized and circulated by the Sikh Heritage Project of the Asian Cultural History Program, Smithsonian Institution. Venues (to 2013): National Museum of Natural History, Smithsonian Institution (Washington, D.C.), July 24, 2004 – October 3, 2007. Santa Barbara Museum of Natural History (Santa Barbara, California), February 21 – May 1, 2009. Fresno Art Museum (Fresno, California), January 19 – April 30, 2012. Next scheduled venue: Institute of Texan Cultures / University of Texas, San Antonio (2015).

Cataloging-in-Publication Data

Taylor, Paul Michael, 1953- author.
   Sikhs : legacy of the Punjab / Paul Michael Taylor,
Robert Pontsioen.
   — First edition.
     pages ; cm
   Includes bibliographical references.
   ISBN-13: 978-1-891739-90-3
   1. Sikhism—History—Exhibitions. 2. Sikh arts—Exhibitions.
3. Sikhs—History—Exhibitions. I. Pontsioen, Robert, 1978-
author. II. National Museum of Natural History (U.S.). Asian
Cultural History Program. III. Title.
   BL2017.6.T39

Authors' note:
Measurements for objects in the exhibition are given in centimeters. Unless otherwise noted, a single measurement indicates diameter or maximum dimension (height or length); otherwise the information on the dimensions is ordered as follows: height by width by depth.

CONTENTS

Sikhs
Legacy of the Punjab

Golden Temple

INTRODUCTION: SIKH HERITAGE AT THE SMITHSONIAN

This book attempts to provide an introduction to the Sikhs, and to their art and history, for the "general reader" or broad public. The authors dare to attempt such a feat only because we here carefully follow the outlines of a very popular and well-received exhibition which has that same aim and mission and which was developed through years of community involvement and effective co-curatorship. Millions of visitors, first at the Smithsonian's National Museum of Natural History, then at the Santa Barbara Museum of Natural History and later at the Fresno Art Museum, have had the opportunity to see and appreciate the exhibition *Sikhs: Legacy of the Punjab*, through its core text and unchanging sequence of thematic presentations as well as through its regular rotations and transformations, as new artworks were added or substituted. With the encouragement and support of the many benefactors of the exhibition and of the wider Smithsonian "Sikh Heritage Project" (of which the exhibition forms one part), we present this book as a permanent record not only of the exhibition, but also of the shared efforts by so many people working together that produced it.

◀ Fig. 6. North entrance to the exhibition
Sikhs: Legacy of the Punjab at the
Smithsonian's National Museum of Natural
History, Washington, D.C. (2004)

Fig. 7. *Janamsakhi*
Handmade paper, leather binding and cloth cover, 13 x 17 x 6.7
19th century
Courtesy of the Kapany Collection of Sikh Art

One of Sikhism's most important literary traditions is the *Janamsakhi*, a collection of
stories about Guru Nanak's life and travels. There are many variations, and some are
illustrated. This book is hand-written in *Gurmukhi*, the sacred script of the Sikhs. The
binding on this book was replaced and the page size altered at a later date.

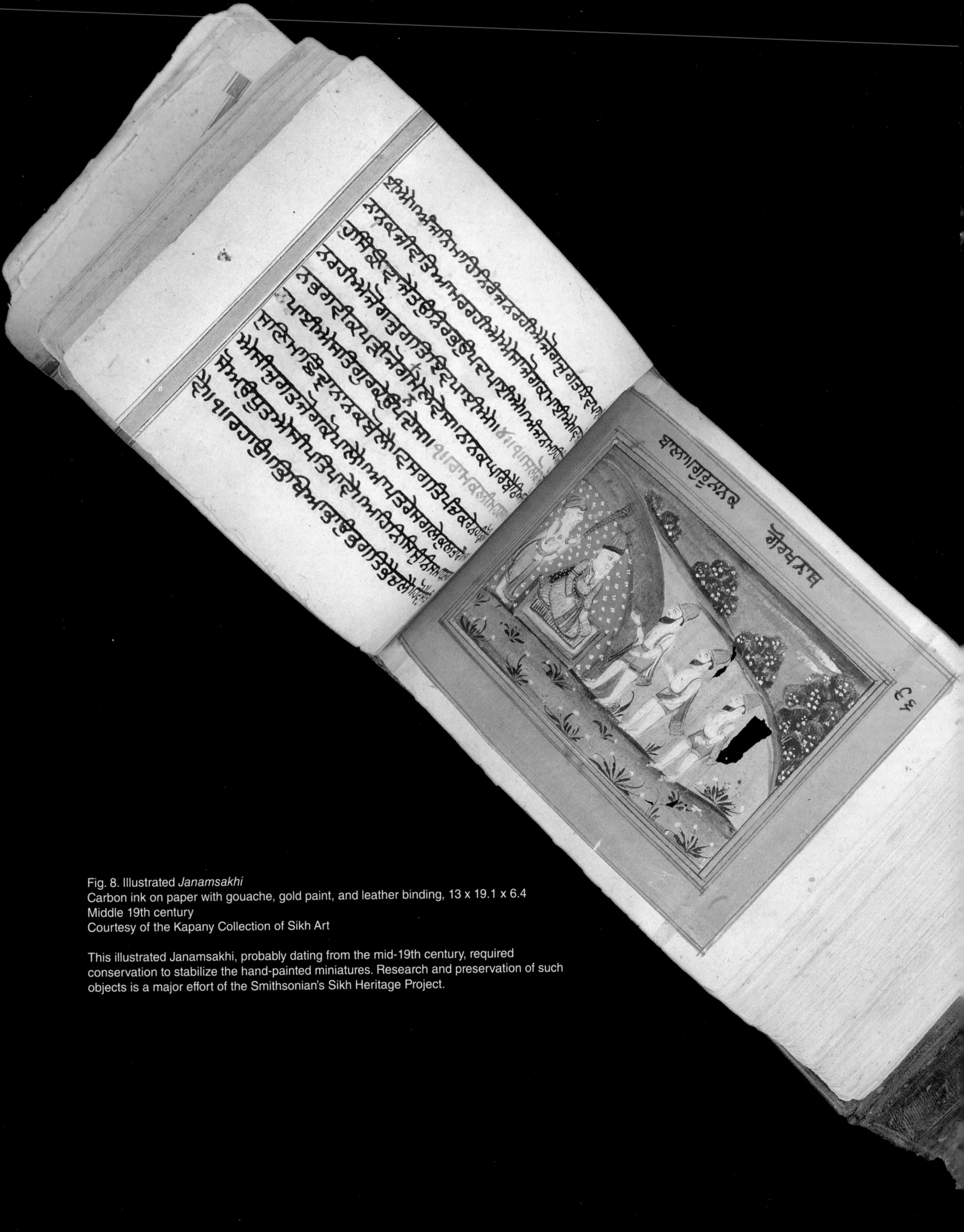

Fig. 8. Illustrated *Janamsakhi*
Carbon ink on paper with gouache, gold paint, and leather binding, 13 x 19.1 x 6.4
Middle 19th century
Courtesy of the Kapany Collection of Sikh Art

This illustrated Janamsakhi, probably dating from the mid-19th century, required conservation to stabilize the hand-painted miniatures. Research and preservation of such objects is a major effort of the Smithsonian's Sikh Heritage Project.

The Smithsonian's Sikh Heritage Project, founded in early 2000, was defined in its founding document as an integrated program of exhibitions, research, collection improvement, and public programs; thus any exhibition envisioned was only one component of the Project's potential scope. In fact, in accepting the first community donations to establish this locus of Sikh heritage activities, the Smithsonian never guaranteed or promised a resulting exhibition. Yet by 2004, the very effective series of lectures, performances, and targeted research trips had grown into a successful new exhibition which benefitted from the involvement and suggestions of many participants who had watched the project grow from its inception. Stepping outside the process to observe it, one sees that the frequent successful events, and other highly visible public activities, serve as a good example of how museums (like universities and other components of contemporary public culture) do produce events that are "rituals" in the anthropological sense, as such public rituals serve to assert the importance of the shared values of a community that gathers for these events. However, the goals of these events and of this exhibition included a strong component of educational outreach to the large non-Sikh population, who would come to understand Sikh identity better through a prominent and visually compelling, highly public exhibition about Sikh heritage.

One purpose of this book is to provide a preliminary account of how a very active South Asian American community became involved in a unique collaboration that produced several positive outcomes (including this exhibition) at relatively modest cost and within a comparatively short period of time. In this case, museum and other institutional goals came (over time) to coincide in part with community goals, and with the research interests of scholars based at the Museum and elsewhere.

In this way, the Sikh Heritage Project and the exhibition described in this book have attempted to seek and to integrate community involvement in ways well beyond the norm in contemporary museum work; in fact, an active group of community members was involved even in the early decision of whether to focus our collective effort toward exhibition or toward other potential goals of the Project.

At the outset, that decision was far from unanimous. Some felt that the Smithsonian should prioritize other goals such as preservation of artifacts that were already on exhibition or in museum collections in India, but which badly needed specialized conservation work for their preservation. Others pointed to the potential for new publications, or assistance with other forms of education such as public lectures. Indeed through the years since its founding in 2000, the Sikh Heritage Project has addressed in part all these goals, through a series of annual lectures and through efforts to assist conservation of artifacts as well as major structures such as the Qila Mubarak in Patiala, India. In 2006 the Sikh Heritage Project co-hosted, in conjunction with the Anandpur Sahib Foundation and the government of the Punjab, a conference on the application of new technologies in the field of cultural heritage preservation for the Punjab. Supported in part by the Indo-US Science and Technology Commission, our conference was memorable partly for bringing together scholars from both Pakistan and India, from Western and Eastern Punjab, to jointly address issues of heritage preservation. More recently, the Sikh Heriage Project and the (independent) Sikh Heritage Foundation (based in Weirton, West Virginia) contributed toward the production of *Sikh Heritage: Ethos & Relics* (Sikhandar Singh and Roopinder Singh, New Delhi: Rupa, 2012), a uniquely important volume of perspectives on the material heritage of the Sikhs in the Punjab today (Taylor 2012).

So undoubtedly there was much else to do in the name of Sikh Heritage, besides an exhibition. But after the events of September 11, 2001, misunderstanding and mis-identification was rife in America, and the need for greater awareness and understanding about Sikhs became much more acute than previously (Alag 2005; Yeager et al.

Fig. 9. Conservator Hanna Szczepanowska stabilizing a fragile gouache on paper painting. (2004)

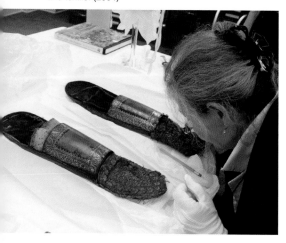

Fig. 10. Metal conservator Betty Siefert restores a historic Sikh arm guard of metal and textile. (2004)

Fig. 11. A conservator carefully repairs the chainmail of a ceremonial Sikh helmet. (2004)

2007). This was also recognized by the Sikh community, which threw its support behind the idea of a major exhibition on the Sikhs at the Smithsonian; and recognized also within the Smithsonian, which moved the production of this exhibition onto a fast track (by the normal standards of exhibition production). It may be added, merely as a point of historical interest now, that at that time the Museum also had a long-term plan for the construction of a new permanent hall of Asian peoples, within a series of regional cultural halls (a plan later abandoned). As curator for Asian, European, and Middle Eastern cultures, Paul Taylor proposed that the Hall be constructed in component parts, with the exhibition on Sikhs as one part of the hall and a Korea Gallery as a second part, to be followed by a series of others. (In fact only those two were actually completed before the overall plan for cultural halls was abandoned; the Sikh exhibition opened in 2004 and the Korea Gallery in 2007, see Taylor and Lotis 2008.)

When one considers the wide range of standard curatorial tasks and responsibilities, including such didactic or educational functions of curatorial work as the selection of themes and objects, or the choice of appropriate modes of interpretation, this project encompassed many examples of co-curatorship with a large community that arrived at and presented decisions in a process quite separate from a traditional museum-based development process.

This involvement of an active Sikh community of supporters, scholars, and interested observers has, somewhat inadvertently, helped to turn a Museum space into a public, multi-generational gathering space for a broad and diverse Sikh or Punjabi-American community. Each museum hosting this exhibition became a place where inspiring Sikh events also regularly occurred , and a place of national public recognition for Sikhs at a time of perceived threats and hardship resulting from public misunderstanding in the post-September 11th period. Even the statement jointly issued within the U.S. Congress on the occasion of the exhibition's opening, by the Co-chairs of the India Caucus (U.S. Representative Joseph Crowley of New York and Representative Joe Wilson of South Carolina), congratulated "the Sikh Community and the Smithsonian Institution for coming together to establish a Sikh Gallery and a Sikh Heritage Project at the National Museum of Natural History" and commending all involved "for having made this honorable endeavor possible." [1]

Finally, from the perspective of museum practice, it is interesting to note the extent to which Sikh community values affected normal museum practices. For example, the idea of organizing anything like a "V.I.P. reception" in conjunction with openings or other events for this exhibition seems to have clashed with the strong Sikh ethos of egalitarianism. In addition, though there were individual Sikh donors who may have been financially able to support the entire exhibition, or other entire components of the Sikh Heritage Project's activities, this was never the preferred method of funding any such activity. Such tasks were always best accomplished through bringing together a larger number of people who would function like a community, all willingly and jointly contributing to the same cause, in a way consistent with each person's abilities.

Thus through the numerous gatherings and meetings for the development of this exhibition and all its associated lectures, events, or performances, we have observed the Sikh community's frequently expressed attempts to make sure that everyone who wished to do so could find a way to contribute something. As museum or exhibition curators we also observed that many of the best ideas for potential exhibit themes, or for the objects and images that could illustrate such themes, came from these meetings. In this way the story this exhibition and book tells to introduce the Sikhs emerges out of the collaborative effort of many narrators working together.

Fig. 12. A set of 24 watercolor paintings on ivory, including this magnificent portrait of Maharaja Ranjit Singh, required extensive conservation and stabilization which was carried out by conservator Hanna Szczepanowska. Conservation work in conjunction with an exhibition also ensures the long-term preservation of fragile Sikh art. (2004)

Fig. 13. Installation of some of the ivory portraits in the exhibition at the Smithsonian. The ivory portrait of Maharaja Ranjit Singh can be seen above. Watercolors on ivory are among the most light-sensitive of artworks, thus their display was limited to just a few months (depending on light level), and then other objects took their place. For the preservation of such fragile artworks, some sections of the exhibition required frequent "rotation," or substitutions using different artworks. (2004)

---

[1] "News Release" by Rep. Joseph Crowley (dated July 25, 2004), "Congressman Joesph Crowley Commends Opening of First Ever Sikh Gallery at Smithsonian Institution"; "Statement for Immediate Release" by Rep. Joe Wilson (dated July 24, 2004), "Wilson Applauds Opening of Sikh Exhibit at Smithsonian," distributed.

AGE OF THE SIKH GURUS

Early in the 16th century, Guru Nanak, a teacher and visionary who lived in the Punjab, began sharing his beliefs about God and equality among all peoples. Instead of emphasizing ritual practices, Guru Nanak offered advice about daily life. His simple message of hard work, ethical living, and seeking knowledge of the divine attracted many followers. Nine subsequent Gurus expanded Nanak's teachings and contributed their own. In this way, Sikhism slowly grew in the Punjab and the Sikhs emerged as a distinct group of people.

The first three Sikh Gurus named one of their disciples based upon their service, convictions, and beliefs. Subsequent Gurus chose successors from within their own families who exhibited these same qualities (Cheema 2010; Duggal 2006; and Singh, Dalip 1999). This chapter explores the early history of Sikhism through a look at the formative years during which the Sikh Gurus lived. Particular focus is placed, within this summary, on Guru Nanak and Guru Gobind Singh and the important role they played in the development of the Sikh religion.

◀ Fig. 14. *The Ten Gurus and Guru Gobind Singh's Four Sons*
Artist Unknown
Gouache on paper, 20.6 x 16.6
Early 19th century
Courtesy of the Kapany Collection of Sikh Art

The Sikh Gurus and their years of leadership:
Center (top to bottom):
Guru Nanak (1469–1539)
Guru Gobind Singh (1675–1708)

Left side (top to bottom):
Guru Angad (1539–1552)
Guru Amar Das (1552–1574)
Guru Ram Das (1574–1581)
Guru Arjan (1581–1606)

Right side (top to bottom):
Guru Har Gobind (1606–1644)
Guru Har Rai (1644–1661)
Guru Har Krishan (1661–1664)
Guru Tegh Bahadur (1664–1675)

Guru Nanak, the First Guru (1469–1539)

Born in the small Punjabi village of Talwandi (now in Pakistan), Guru Nanak grew up in a Hindu family. According to Sikh traditions, at age thirty he mysteriously disappeared from a river where he was bathing. When he returned three days later, Guru Nanak spoke about his powerful religious experience and about how God values the way people live more than the religion they followed (Singh, Khushwant 2004; Nesbitt and Kaur 1999).

Fig. 15. *Guru Nanak*
Sobha Singh (1901-1986)
Oil on masonite, 89.5 x 73.7
1969
Gifted by Dr. R.K. Janmeja Singh for the
Kapany Collection of Sikh Art

This painting by renowned Sikh artist
Sobha Singh honors the 500-year birth
anniversary of Guru Nanak, the first Sikh
Guru. Many Sikhs hang reproductions of
famous Guru portraits in their homes.

Although he was born into a family of Hindus, Guru Nanak challenged aspects of Hindu and Islamic practices and began to develop a new religious understanding. This was the foundation of the Sikh religion, and Guru Nanak's nine successor Gurus developed Guru Nanak's followers into a cohesive community with its own literature, beliefs, art, traditions, and institutions.

Stories handed down from generation to generation recount that Guru Nanak traveled extensively for the next 20 years. Over time, more and more people came to listen to his teachings and songs. Guru Nanak composed more than 900 hymns that are part of the Sikh holy book, the Guru Granth Sahib (Singh, Khushwant 2008).

Fig. 16. Map illustrating the places Guru Nanak is reported to have visited.

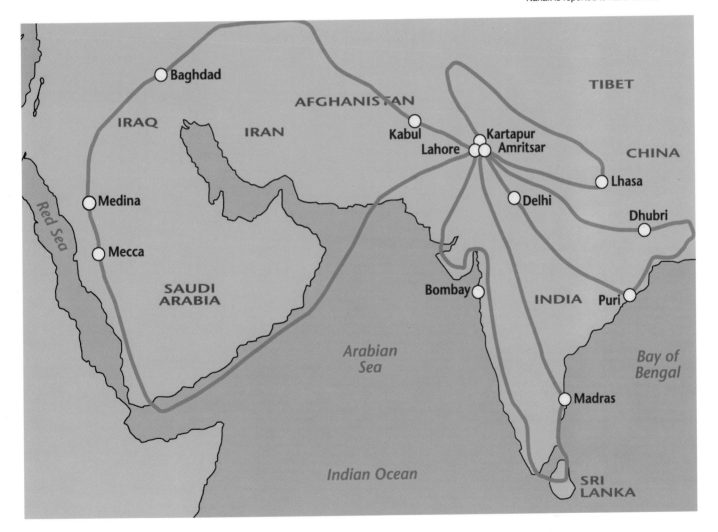

Fig. 17. *Guru Nanak with Mardana and Bala*
Artist Unknown
Gouache, gold paint, glass beads, mirror, and gesso on teak board, 59 x 75.5
Early 20th century
Courtesy of Dr. Anmol S. Mahal and Dr. Surjit K. Mahal

The halo encircling Guru Nanak's head and the fly whisk are characteristic symbols of reverence in portraits of the ten Sikh Gurus. The canopy protects Guru Nanak and his two companions, Mardana and Bala. In this style of Indian painting, called *Tanjore,* artists create a relief-like surface with gesso, and then add gouache, decorative glass, and gold paint. This piece probably dates from the early 19th century and was retouched in recent years.

The Second through Ninth Gurus

Despite having two sons of his own, Guru Nanak chose as his successor one of his most humble and devoted followers, who was named Lehna but became known as Guru Angad (1504-52). Guru Angad is often credited with collecting the hymns composed by Guru Nanak and developing the Gurmukhi script in which the sacred Sikh scripture was originally recorded.

Fig. 18. Visitors enjoy a communal meal (*langar*) in Amritsar, Punjab, India. (June 2006)

Guru Angad named as his successor a Hindu convert named Amar Das (1479-1574) who became a devout follower of Guru Nanak's teachings. Guru Amar Das is most often credited with organizing the Sikh community into a cohesive society and with establishing *langar*, which had been first developed by Guru Nanak, as a key Sikh institution (Singh and Singh 2012: 34). Langar is the dining hall or community kitchen attached to all Sikh gurdwaras at which all visitors, regardless of age, religion, rank or class, sit down and share a free meal together as equals. The word also refers to the meal served there.

The fourth Guru, Guru Ram Das (1534-81), was the son-in-law of Guru Amar Das and is particularly remembered for founding the city of Amritsar, which remains the holiest site of the Sikh religion. Guru Ram Das named his youngest son, Arjan, as his successor and it was up to Guru Arjan (1563-1606) to begin construction of a major house of prayer at Amritsar. This house of worship was known as Darbar Sahib (and to tourists as the Golden Temple). As explained in the next chapter, Guru Arjan was also responsible for compiling the teachings of the Gurus into the Guru Granth Sahib, or Sikh scripture, for the first time. Upon the death of the Mughal Emperor Akbar in 1605, the growing influence and unity of the Sikh community came to be perceived as a threat by Akbar's son Jahangir, who had Guru Arjan arrested, tortured and killed.

After the martyrdom of Guru Arjan, his son Hargobind became the sixth Sikh Guru during a period in which the Sikhs were increasingly oppressed by the ruling Mughal Empire. For this reason, Hargobind's period as Guru saw an increased militarism within the Sikh community. Guru Hargobind named his grandson as his successor, who became the seventh Guru, named Guru Har

Rai (1630-61), at the age of fourteen. Before he died at age 31, he named his five year-old son, Harkrishan, as his successor and eighth Guru. Guru Harkrishan (1656-1664) was widely known as an enlightened boy with an understanding of the Guru Granth Sahib that belied his tender age. Before he died at the age of eight, he named his uncle (and son of Guru Hargobind) as his successor and ninth Guru.

Guru Tegh Bahadur (1621-75) was a celebrated Sikh warrior but is best known for tirelessly promoting the causes of peace and religious tolerance and for contributing many hymns to the Guru Granth Sahib. In 1675, Guru Tegh Bahadur was arrested for refusing to convert to Islam and was later executed by the Mughal Emperor Aurangzeb. For his sacrifice, Guru Tegh Bahadur is widely respected for defending not only the Sikh religion, but also the universal right to practice any faith one chooses. Before his martyrdom, Guru Tegh Bahadur named his son as his successor; that son was Guru Gobind Singh (1666-1708).

Guru Gobind Singh, the Tenth Guru (1666–1708)

Gobind Singh, son of the ninth Guru, was one of the most influential Sikh Gurus as well as the last living Guru. Named a guru at age nine, he is remembered for strengthening the Sikh community. To unite Sikhs and emphasize their equality, he gave all Sikh men the surname Singh, which means "lion," and all Sikh women the surname Kaur, meaning "princess." Sikhs still use these names today, often along with other surnames, to express their devotion to the Sikh principles of equality and respect for all people regardless of status or gender.

Fig. 19. *Guru Gobind Singh*
Gursewak Singh (b. 1951)
Oil on canvas, 44.5 x 59
2004

Portraits of Guru Gobind Singh and other historical subjects are a popular art tradition in the Punjab. This vividly colored portrait and the two works to the right are typical of art found in Sikh homes and places of worship. Guru Gobind Singh usually appears with a hawk, a symbol of authority.

In 1699, Guru Gobind Singh called for volunteers willing to give their lives for their faith. The five men who came forward became known as the Five Beloveds (usually depicted today in matching blue turbans and tunics). Arguably, Guru Gobind Singh's foremost accomplishment was the founding of the Khalsa, or elevation of the Sikh community to the Khalsa, which served to galvanize the community's members. Ultimately, he shifted his political authority to this community and transferred his spiritual role to the sacred book. Thereafter, Sikhs saw themselves as a community and a people who followed the writings compiled by the Gurus (Singh, Preetam 2000).

Through the installation of the collected Sikh scripture, the Guru Granth Sahib, as his successor in 1708, Guru Gobind Singh ended the line of human Gurus. Ever since Guru Gobind Singh's declaration that the Guru Granth Sahib should be the last and eternal living Guru, the Guru Granth Sahib has been accorded the same respect and is as central to Sikh devotions and daily life as were the first ten Gurus.

Fig. 21. *Guru Gobind Singh Receiving Amrit*
Gursewak Singh (b. 1951)
Oil on canvas, 44.5 x 59
2004

This pair of paintings shows Gobind Singh giving the Five Beloveds *amrit,* a sweetened water. Then, in a gesture demonstrating Sikh views on equality, the Guru begs the Five for them to give him the blessing of *amrit.*

Fig. 20. *Guru Gobind Singh Giving Amrit to the Five Beloveds*
Gursewak Singh (b. 1951)
Oil on canvas, 44 x 59.5
2004

GURU GRANTH SAHIB: SIKH SCRIPTURE BECOMES THE ETERNAL GURU

The Sikh holy book, the Guru Granth Sahib, was compiled during the time of the ten Sikh Gurus and is considered to be the successor of the human gurus themselves. The earliest compilation of Sikh scripture was completed by the fifth Guru, Guru Arjan, in the first decade of the seventeenth century and included the writings of not only the first five Gurus but also Muslim, Hindu, and other Sikh holy men and poets. This early compilation was installed in the Gurdwara of the Darbar Sahib by Guru Arjan in 1604 (Cole and Sambhi 1978: 26). The final compilation of Sikh scripture was brought together by the tenth and final human Guru, Guru Gobind Singh, who added the writings of his predecessor, Guru Tegh Bahadur, and installed the scripture as his successor. It is this final compilation that became known as the Guru Granth Sahib and remains the eternal Guru and sacred text of the Sikhs.

◄ Fig. 22. Portable *Palki*
Silver, 13.3 x 6.4 x 6.7
c. 1914-18
Courtesy of the Kapany Collection of Sikh Art

Palki are used to "house" the Guru Granth Sahib. This portable palki contains a miniature holy book and was carried by a soldier during World War I.

Fig. 23. During the service, Sikhs wave a *chouri* (bottom right), an ancient sign of authority, over the holy book. (Silver Spring, Maryland, 2004)

Fig. 24. *Guru Granth Sahib*
29 x 44 x 9
Joseph F. Cullman 3rd Library of Natural
History, Smithsonian Institution

This three-column version of the same
page of the Guru Granth Sahib includes
Gurmukhi script, a Romanization of
Punjabi text, and the English translation.
This kind of text helps to increase the
accessibility of the Guru Granth Sahib as
Sikhism rapidly expands around the world.

Sacred Book
Becomes the Last Guru

The Sikh holy book, the *Guru Granth Sahib*, contains more than 5,800 poetic compositions by six Sikh Gurus, over a dozen Sikh poets, and 15 Muslim and Hindu holy men whose teachings reflect Sikh views.

Together, these writings inspire sacred teachings and offer guidelines for conduct, such as caring for fellow human beings and rising above differences in creed, caste, and race.

left This ph[...] Granth Sahib[...] in Gurmukhi[...] same numbe[...]

below This t[...] the Guru Gra[...] Romanizatio[...]

Sikhs treat their holy book with the same signs of respect that were accorded their living Gurus. During services, it rests on a platform and is protected by a canopy. The *chouri* is waved over the book when it is opened or closed.

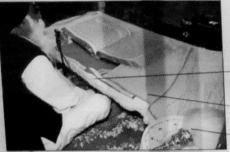

Manji Sahib (throne with cushions) is a place of honor, similar to a maharaja's throne.

Rumalas (ornate cloths) dress their holy book as clothes would a ruler.

Chouri (ceremonial fly whisk) waving is a South Asian sign of respect.

The Guru Granth Sahib contains more than 5,800 poetic compositions by six Sikh Gurus, over a dozen Sikh poets, and 15 Muslim and Hindu holy men whose teachings reflect Sikh views. Together, these writings inspire sacred teachings and offer guidelines for conduct, such as caring for fellow human beings and rising above differences in creed, caste, and race. Sikhs treat their holy book with the same signs of respect that were accorded their living Gurus. During services, it rests on a platform and is protected by a canopy. The *chouri* is waved over the book when it is opened or closed (see Macauliffe 1990; and Singh, Pashaura 2003).

Fig. 25. *Sikhs: Legacy of the Punjab* exhibition display case titled "Sacred Book Becomes the Last Guru"

Sikh tradition requires covering the head and removing shoes when in the company of the holy book, out of respect for its status as the living Guru. Because it was not possible to comply with these practices in a museum environment, the *Sikhs: Legacy of the Punjab* display featuring the Guru Granth Sahib substituted a prop for the holy book as seen in the photo to the left.

THE KHALSA: ARMED WITH TRADITION

Guru Gobind Singh's founding of the Khalsa, or elevation of the community to Khalsa, instilled courage and confidence in the Sikh community and provided them with a vision for the future, under the authority of the holy book. Five symbols, or the Five Ks, give members of the Khalsa a recognizable physical identity.

The Five Ks

Kes (uncut hair) symbolizes the body in a pristine state.

Kangha (comb) is a sign of cleanliness because it keeps hair neat and clean.

Kaccha (breeches) represents a type of short garment once worn by warriors, a sign of self-restraint.

Karha (steel bracelet) stands for one God and strength.

Kirpan (sword) should be raised only to fight injustice.

◄ Fig. 26. *Three Akalis*
Emily Eden (1797-1869)
Colored lithograph
Courtesy of the Kapany Collection of
Sikh Art

The five Ks can be found on these Sikh soldiers, who are known as *Akalis*. They were dedicated defenders of the Sikh faith. Their distinctive turbans often held quoits and other Sikh weapons.

While defending their faith and territory, Sikhs developed a highly respected military tradition that borrowed many styles and materials from other cultures in South Asia. This selection of arms and armor represents weaponry typically used by Sikh warriors (see Madra 1999).

Fig. 27. Ceremonial Sikh Helmet
Gilded copper, 13.5 x 18 x 23.1
c. 1805-1840
Courtesy of the Kapany Collection of Sikh Art

The special shape of this helmet accommodates a Sikh topknot. The two bosses near the topknot would have held plumes or other decorations. Along the bottom, a row of holes would have held protective chain mail.

Fig. 29. *Sikhs: Legacy of the Punjab* ▶ exhibition display case titled "Armed with Tradition"
Armor Set with Helmet, Breast and Side Plates, and Arm Guards
Steel, brass, gold leaf, and velvet
18th century

Sikh soldiers wore similar sets of armor in the wars with the British during the 1840s. On the arm guards of this set, notice the dark gray embroidery and tiny circles (now tarnished silver-wrapped thread and silver sequins)—both signs that this set was intended for ceremonial use.

Fig. 28. Micrograph (high magnification image) of metal arm defense used with Sikh armor, showing gold leaf on metal. Small specks of metal corrosion protrude from beneath the gold leaf, but cannot safely be removed. Nevertheless, careful attention to the display and storage environment prevents further corrosion, thus keeping the armor in a stable condition. Scale at lower right: 5 millimeters. (2004)

Armed with Tradition

While defending their faith and territory, Sikhs developed a highly respected military tradition that borrowed many styles and materials from other cultures in India. This selection of arms and armor represents weaponry typically used by Sikh warriors.

Armor Set with helmet, breast and side plates, and arm guards
Steel, brass, gold leaf, and velvet, ca. 18th century
Loaned by Dr. Sarjit S. Chahil

Sikh soldiers wore similar armor sets in the wars with the British during the 1840s. On the arm guards of this set, notice the dark gray embroidery and tiny circles (now tarnished silver-wrapped thread and silver sequins)—both signs that this set was intended for ceremonial use.

Chakkar (Quoit)
Steel, 20th century
Loaned by Dr. Gurpal S. Bhuller

Sikh soldiers could throw the quoit like a discus with deadly accuracy. For combat, the outer edges of this unique Sikh weapon would be extremely sharp. Sometimes the quoit was worn over a specially shaped turban or hung from a sash.

Katar (Punch dagger)
Tempered and cast steel, ca. late 18th century
Loaned by Dr. Gurpal S. Bhuller

Unique to India, the katar was designed to penetrate armor. The blade is thickest near the point, making it extremely strong. In India, many men wore it tucked in a sash.

Ceremonial Sikh Helmet
Copper with gilt, 1805–1840
Loaned by The Kapany Collection of Sikh Art

The special shape of this helmet accommodates a Sikh topknot. The two bosses near the topknot would have held plumes or other decorations. Along the bottom, a row of holes would have held the protective chain mail. Look for the image of a Hindu deity, an example of the mix of people and religions in the Punjab.

Sword
Steel blade, silver plated hilt, 1720–1790
Loaned by Dr. Gurpal S. Bhuller

The shape and decorative pattern on this sword are typical of the Sikh misal period, in the late 18th century. The inscription along the cutting edge, attributed to Guru Gobind Singh, reads, "You are the One. You are kali. You are the sword, you are the arrow. You are the symbol of victory." The original hilt has been replaced.

Fig. 30. *Katar* (punch dagger) with Cover
Tempered and cast steel, 45.7 x 3.8
Late 18th century
Courtesy of Dr. Gurpal S. Bhuller

Unique to India, the *katar* was designed
to penetrate armor. The blade is thickest
near the point, making it extremely strong.
In India, many men wore it tucked in a
sash.

Fig. 31. *Chakkar* (quoit)
Steel, 25.2 x .2
20th century
Courtesy of Dr. Gurpal S. Bhuller

Sikh soldiers could throw the *chakkar*
like a discus with deadly accuracy. For
combat, the outer edges of this unique
Sikh weapon would be extremely sharp.
Sometimes the quoit was worn over a
specially shaped turban or hung from a
sash.

Fig. 32. Sikh Sword
Steel blade and silver plated hilt,
97.8 x 6.4 (12.7 handle)
c. 1720-1790
Courtesy of Dr. Gurpal S. Bhuller

The shape and decorative pattern on this sword are typical of the Sikh misl period, in the late 18th century. The inscription along the cutting edge, attributed to Guru Gobind Singh, reads in part: "You are the sword, you are the arrow. You are the symbol of victory." The original hilt has been replaced.

Fig. 33. Amrit Bowl and Stirring Sword
Steel
Collection of the Sikh Heritage Foundation

Strengthening the Khalsa

Devout men and women may choose to become dedicated members of the Khalsa or community by attending a simple ceremony. During the ceremony, five Khalsa members, representing the Five Beloveds, recite selections from the scripture and stir sweetened water, called amrit, using a special bowl and a ceremonial sword. The Khalsa members then sprinkle the eyes and hair of the initiate with nectar in a symbolic act pledging equality and faithfulness, and the newly initiated Khalsa members dedicate themselves to the teachings of the ten Gurus and the defense of the downtrodden (Dhillon 1999).

SIKH HERITAGE IN THE PUNJAB

In the decades after Guru Gobind Singh's death, Sikhs endured repeated persecutions for their faith. Conflicts with the Mughals, who ruled India, and with neighboring Afghans, resulted in the deaths of tens of thousands of Sikh men, women, and children. During the early 19th century, however, the Sikh kingdoms rose to prominence and with this increased political power came Sikh courtly traditions of dress and elaborate displays of wealth modeled after the style of India's princely states. The golden era of the Lahore Kingdom ended with the 1845 and 1849 wars against the British. Nearly a century later, the 1947 partitioning of the Punjab to create Pakistan forced many Sikhs to leave their home.

◀ Fig. 34. Statue of Maharaja Ranjit Singh
Artist Unknown, probably from Lahore, Punjab
White marble, 32.1 x 24.5 x 22.1
c. 1900
Courtesy of Drs. Surjit K. and Anmol S. Mahal (The Mahal Family Foundation)

Due to smallpox contracted as a child, Ranjit Singh was blind in one eye, a feature that appears in most portraits of him. The elaborate jewelry he wears, including necklaces and armbands, were an integral part of Sikh courtly dress.

Maharaja Ranjit Singh (1780–1839)

In 1792, twelve-year-old Ranjit Singh assumed leadership of a misl, a group of Sikh military forces. His early military successes, including the capture of Lahore from rival Sikh chiefs, earned him great respect in the Punjab. Ranjit Singh formed a united Sikh kingdom that stopped invaders from the north, expanded Sikh territory, and brought peace and prosperity to that area after nearly a century of turmoil (see Seetal 1970).

By 1800, Ranjit Singh had assumed the political title of Maharaja of the Punjab, although Sikhs represented less than ten percent of the population. During the 40 years of his reign, he created a loyal following due to his reputation for treating all people equally and contributing to both Muslim and Hindu communities. Having contracted smallpox as a child, Ranjit Singh was blind in one eye, a feature that appears in most portraits of him.

Fig. 35. Micrograph (high magnification image) of miniature portrait on ivory shows layering of the paint, along with application of gold leaf, to produce the image seen on the ivory. Scale at lower right: 2 millimeters. (2004)

Fig. 36. Set of Ivory Miniatures ▶
Artist(s) Unknown
Watercolor on ivory
Middle 19th century
Courtesy of the Kapany Collection of Sikh Art

These portraits of the family and court of Ranjit Singh include the white-bearded Maharaja (top-center) and the Europeans who trained his military. Painted ivories such as these were often given to visiting dignitaries.

Early Colonial Encounters

The arrival of the British and other colonial powers in the late 1700s had a dramatic impact on Sikh cultural, military, and aesthetic traditions. Maharaja Ranjit Singh hired European experts to train his armies, and many local artisans adopted Western styles of painting and perspective. Although the Sikhs allied initially with the British, the early agreements dissolved with the death of Ranjit Singh in 1839. Between 1845 and 1849, the British waged two wars against the Sikhs and ultimately gained control of the Punjab.

The most influential of Maharaja Ranjit Singh's wives, Rani Jindan became the symbol of Sikh dignity after her husband died. She posed for this portrait in England, where her son had been taken by the British and had been living since 1854. The portrait captures her daring and defiance. After Rani Jindan escaped British imprisonment to Nepal, the government of India confiscated many of her possessions, including Sikh court jewels.

Fig. 37. Portrait of Rani Jindan
George Richmond (1809-1896)
Oil on board, 74.3 x 58.4
1863
Courtesy of the Kapany Collection of Sikh Art

Fig. 38. Necklace Belonging to Rani Jindan in Box
Diamonds, pearls, rubies, and emeralds, 12.7 x 20.3
Early 19th century
Courtesy of the Kapany Collection of Sikh Art

After Rani Jindan escaped to Nepal, the government of India confiscated many Sikh court jewels. In this necklace, the center gem is an uncut emerald polished in the Indian style. Eleven double-sided clusters are set with rubies and emeralds on the outside and diamonds and enamel on the reverse.

Maharaja Sher Singh, riding the elephant in the image below, was the third son of Ranjit Singh. After his father died, he reigned briefly as maharaja (1841–1843). Sher Singh befriended the artist Alexis Soltykoff, a Russian prince, who sketched many scenes during his travels in India. Sher Singh and his son (in white on the other elephant) were murdered by rival Sikh chiefs in 1843, after which Dalip Singh was declared Maharaja of the Sikh Empire at the age of five with Rani Jindan serving as Regent.

Maharaja Dalip Singh handed over the Sikh kingdom to Sir Henry Hardinge in 1846. The British sent Dalip Singh first to India's United Provinces, where he converted to Christianity, and then to a lavish estate in England, where he mingled freely with British royalty. Dalip Singh was the last in the line of hereditary Maharajas of Lahore (see Seetal 1970; Sidhu 2010).

Fig. 39. Chir Singh (Sher Singh)
Prince Alexis Soltykoff (1806-59)
Lithograph, 51.7 x 69.5
1842
Courtesy of the Kapany Collection of
Sikh Art

Sikhs of the Punjab Today

Throughout their history, Punjabi Sikhs, like Sikhs throughout the world, have preserved their identity despite changing circumstances and forms of government. Pakistan separated from India in 1947 and the new border bifurcated the Sikh homeland, causing Sikhs great heartache and loss of life and property. About 10 million people relocated—Sikhs left Pakistan for India and Muslims moved from India to Pakistan (Jodhka 2010).

> One Sikh remembers: *"There were caravans of men, women, and children walking on foot with their household belongings. A few buses with army escorts would come every day, and masses of Hindus and Sikhs would rush to get into these buses. This continued for several weeks. Every day, we would return disappointed. It was a lucky day when all of us managed to get into a bus and finally reach India."* (Anonymous, Maryland, 2004)

Who are the modern Sikhs? Once, it was easy to describe Sikhs as a people primarily from the Punjab region. However, as Sikhs emigrated around the world and Sikhism continued to attract new followers, Sikhs became an increasingly diverse group. Uniting most Sikhs is that they identify daily meditation on God, honest work, and service to the community as the central themes of their faith. When describing themselves, many refer to what the Punjabis call *chardi kala*, an expression of optimism in the face of adversity (see Oberoi 1994; Singh, Sardar Kapur 2000).

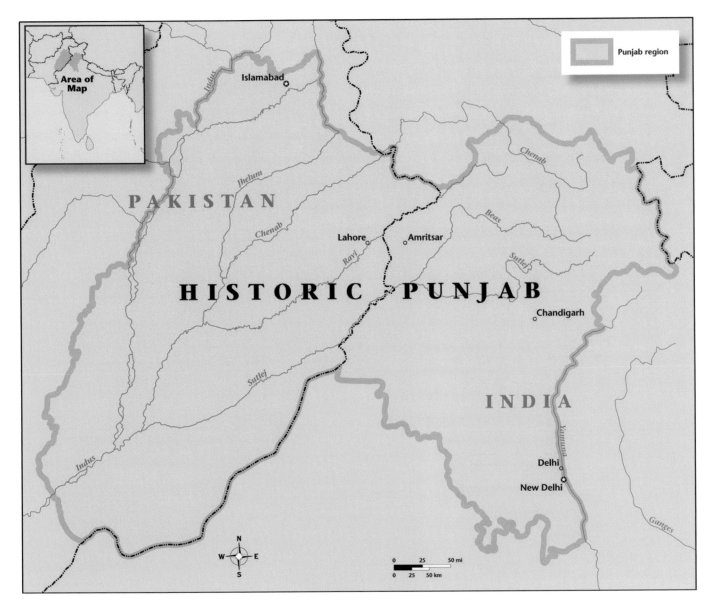

Fig. 40. Pakistan separated from India in 1947. As shown in the map above, the border split the Sikh homeland of the Punjab.

THE PRACTICE OF SIKH FAITH

How Do Sikhs Celebrate?

Sikhs rejoice in a distinctively Punjabi way. Their prayers, food, music, and dance all reflect the Punjabi culture—a lively mix of religions, customs and people. Sikhs distinguish their celebrations by including prayers and readings from the Guru Granth Sahib. This chapter briefly outlines several major annual Sikh holidays and festivals, the Sikh wedding ceremony and celebration, and some of the ways in which Sikhs practice their faith.

◀ Fig. 41. Sikh celebrants enter the Darbar Sahib. (June 2006)

Sikh Holidays and Festivals

Gurpurbs

These religious holidays celebrate the lives of the Gurus and are usually marked at Sikh places of worship by reading aloud the entire Guru Granth Sahib.

Hola Mahalla (February/March)

During this weeklong festival, Sikhs gather to compete in mock sword fights and other martial arts displays, perform music, and engage in poetry contests. A parade, community feast, and prayers for health complete this festival which was first celebrated by the tenth Guru, Guru Gobind Singh in 1700 (Singh, Gurbachan 1998: 90).

Vaisakhi (mid-April)

Celebrated in the spring, this annual feast commemorates the founding of the Khalsa with lively and colorful fairs. A new Sikh flag is raised at every gurdwara.

Diwali (early November)

This celebration honors the sixth Sikh Guru, Guru Hargobind, with the lighting of candles at home and at the gurdwara. The festival commemorates Guru Hargobind's return to his community after wrongful imprisonment.

Fig. 42. Sikh devotee at the Darbar Sahib, Amritsar, Punjab, India. (June 2006)

THE PRACTICE OF SIKH FAITH [61]

The Sikh Wedding

The Sikh wedding is a simple religious ceremony. The four *lavan* (hymns) are recited as the couple walks around the holy book four times—each circle signifying a different aspect of married and spiritual life (see Kaur Singh and Kaur Singh 1999). Before the wedding, the bride's female relatives gather to bathe her and adorn her hands and feet with henna, and the bride's family hosts a gathering where women dance, play the *dholki* (drum), and sing songs that poke fun at the groom and his family.

During the ceremony the bride's father places one end of a scarf held by the groom, into his daughter's hands. The gesture recognizes the bride's new connection to the groom and his family, and the union of the families. After the ceremony, guests and family congratulate the bride and shower her with gifts and blessings.

Sikh Groom and Bridal Clothing and Jewelry

Women typically wear *salwar*, a pair of loose-fitting pants, and a *kamiz*, or tunic, during the wedding service. The *chunni* covers the bride's head during the service. The bride may change into a matching skirt at the reception or other events. Specially embroidered shoes are traditional.

Sikh grooms typically wear a long, embroidered jacket called a *sherwani*. The color and fabric of the shawl and turban often coordinates with the bride's wedding outfit.

Today, Sikh brides combine traditional styles and family heirlooms with contemporary pieces. The bride's uncle and aunt traditionally give red and white plastic bracelets, called *churra*, to the bride.

Fig. 43. Detail of *Sikhs: Legacy of the Punjab* exhibition display case titled "How do Sikhs Celebrate?"

On left:
Sherwani, Shawl, and Turban
Early 20th century
Courtesy of Dr. Sohan S. and Mrs. Kamal K. Chaudhry

On right:
Salwar, Kamiz, and *Chunni*
Silk brocade and chiffon with *dabaka* embroidery
20th century
Courtesy of Samyukt Sandhu

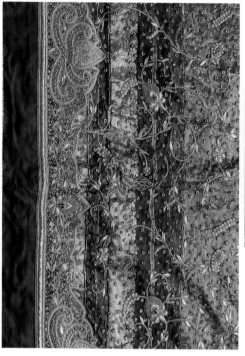

Fig. 44. Wedding objects courtesy of: The Malik Family, Mr. Gurinder Singh and Mrs. Harsharon Singh, Mr. Sandeep Singh and Mrs. Pinky Singh, Mr. Japdeep Singh and Mrs. Roshni Singh, Paulina Ledergerber-Crespo, and Ganga Singh Dhillon.

How Do Sikhs Practice Their Faith?

Private Reverence

So important is daily devotion to God that many Sikh homes include a separate prayer room with a copy of the Guru Granth Sahib. The room provides a refuge during difficult times and an inspiration in moments of joy. At sunrise, sunset, and just before bed, Sikhs recite prayers and read from the Guru Granth Sahib. Every morning, Sikhs take out the book to read and then return it to a resting place at night.

Fig. 45. A Sikh woman reads from the Guru Granth Sahib in the privacy of her prayer room. As acts of respect, Sikhs remove their shoes and cover their heads in the presence of their holy book. (May 2004)

Seeking Daily Guidance

Many Sikhs looking for daily advice practice *hukam*, in which they turn randomly to a page in the Guru Granth Sahib and read the first hymn on the left side. During the day, Sikhs reflect on the message of the hymn.

Gathering Together

The Sikh place of worship, or gurdwara, reflects Sikh tenets and Punjabi customs. Most important, a Sikh service features a prominent display of their holy book, the Guru Granth Sahib. Traditionally, men and women sit separately because of a Punjabi practice discouraging casual touching between genders.

The Sikh Turban

The Sikh turban is the most common way to recognize a Sikh male. Sikh men cover their hair, even during sleep and sports, to keep it clean, a custom originating with the tenth Guru. At weddings, male family members may exchange turban lengths in a gesture of friendship. The eldest son receives turbans when his father dies in recognition of the new position within the family (see Manukhani 2004).

Raising Sikh Youth

Like many immigrant groups in the U.S., Sikhs often send their children to special schools and camps. Sikh schools are often associated with local gurdwaras and teach children the Gurmukhi script and Sikh history. These schools give children a sense of community and fellowship.

Service to Community

Most Sikhs identify seva, or service to the community, as a central theme of their faith. This can include working together to clean the sacred pool at the Darbar Sahib (see Figure 55), helping to prepare or serve the langar meal at a local Gurdwara (Figure 47), and many other forms of service to community.

Fig. 46. As a sign of respect, Sikhs hold the holy book above their heads when it is moved. (Silver Spring, Maryland, May 2004)

Fig. 47. Sikhs take turns preparing and serving a vegetarian meal, called langar, after the service. (Silver Spring, Maryland, May 2004)

Fig. 48. Members of a Sikh family wear various turban and chunni (head covering) styles at the entrance to the Darbar Sahib. (June 2006)

Fig. 49. Volunteer teacher Shalini Chugh teaches the Beginning Punjabi class (for seven-year-old children) at a Sikh Sunday school held at a Gurdwara in Fresno, California. Her students follow a general American school education during the week but meet on Sundays to study the Punjabi language and Sikh history and religion. (January 2012)

Fig. 50. Volunteer student assistant
Mehek Kaur gives extra help with Punjabi
language study to a younger student,
Zorawar Singh, at a Sikh Sunday school
in Fresno, California. (January 2012)

DARBAR SAHIB

The Sikh Holy Space

The most historically and politically significant site for the Sikh community, the *Darbar Sahib* (popularly known in English as the Golden Temple) shines as a symbol of Sikh heritage and faith. Located in Amritsar, India near the Pakistan border, the Darbar Sahib has drawn Sikh pilgrims and other area residents since its construction in the late 16th century.

During the mid-1700s, invading armies destroyed the building several times, but each time the Sikhs rebuilt the Temple. The existing structure, a blend of Hindu and Muslim architectural styles, dates back to the 1760s. The gilding was applied in 1802 during Maharaja Ranjit Singh's rule (see Singh, Harbans 1999).

◄ Fig. 51. Inside the Darbar Sahib ("Golden Temple"), Amritsar, Punjab, India. (June 2006)

Fig. 52. Model of Darbar Sahib
Devinder Singh (b. 1947)
Gold leaf and mixed media
2004
Courtesy of the Sikh Heritage Foundation
(Wierton, WV) through a gift by the Malik
Family in honor of Sikh martyrs.

This striking model, commissioned for
the exhibition, stands as a work of art on
its own and forms a visually compelling
centerpiece.

Fig. 53. Detail of model of Darbar Sahib

Fig. 54. A Sikh woman and boy walk
around the Darbar Sahib. (June 2006)

Fig. 55. *Kar Sewa*
Sukhpreet Singh (b. 1969)
Oil on canvas, 100.4 x 182
2004
Courtesy of the Kapany Collection of
Sikh Art

In this richly detailed painting by
contemporary Sikh artist Sukhpreet
Singh, hundreds of Sikhs collaborate to
clean the sacred pool as a form of *seva,*
or service, to their community.

Fig. 56. Temple Tokens
Copper or Silver
Late 19th century – Early 20th century
Courtesy of Dr. Gurpal S. Bhuller

These tokens were once given to pilgrims
who made an offering to the gurdwara.

My Visit to the Darbar Sahib

"Hundreds of Sikhs jostled beside me, but I felt I was on a journey all by myself. Inside, there was splendor all around. As I knelt before the Guru Granth Sahib ji, my mind emptied and a prayer rose from the recesses of my heart, a prayer thanking Him for the blessings He has showered upon me. My prayer asked for strength to live my life righteously, to love my fellow humankind equally, to do seva *[service], and to dwell on and remember His name constantly.*

I touched my forehead to the ground, letting the tranquility enter my body. I was humbled by the sacrifice of those who have gone before me so that I may live my life in comfort today. As I left, I felt spiritually renewed and connected with those around me. I walked with supreme joy and peace."

—Anonymous, Maryland, 2004

Fig. 57. At night, the lights and reflections of the Darbar Sahib create a magical and inspiring vision. (June 2006)

The Darbar Sahib and 1984

The presence of two contemporary Sikh artworks with the title "1984" in the exhibit *Sikhs: Legacy of the Punjab* required explanation of the date's significance. Here there was especially heated disagreement in how this subject-matter should be handled within the exhibition context. Originally we had intended to include, among the photo panels surrounding the central scale model of the Darbar Sahib, a narrative with photos of the 1984 Operation Bluestar attack. This elicited strong negative reaction among those who felt that the central model should be uplifting and focused on the religious experience of the place. In the end, everyone accepted that a simple label should be placed near each of the "1984" contemporary paintings in the gallery of rotating artworks, for which curator Paul Taylor proposed the following text (as corrected by numerous suggestions from among those to whom it was circulated):

Sikhs and 1984

Works by contemporary Sikh artists outside the Punjab often commemorate the Amritsar tragedy of June, 1984 and its aftermath. In "Operation Bluestar," Indian troops attempted to displace a group of Sikh nationalists, who were inside the sacred Darbar Sahib (Golden Temple) complex. The attack left many dead and damaged sacred Sikh buildings. These events and the October 31, 1984 assassination of Prime Minister Indira Gandhi by her Sikh bodyguards triggered civil unrest that resulted in the arrests and deaths of many Sikhs.

These contemporary oil paintings by the Singh Twins (page 78) and Arpana Caur (page 79) have been among the most popular artworks for Sikh and non-Sikh viewers of the exhibition. The rotating artwork areas in which they were displayed also allowed for the exploration of other themes within the broad scope of Sikh heritage.

Fig. 58. *1984 (The Storming of the "Golden Temple")*
The Singh Twins (b. 1966)
Gouache and gold dust on mount board,
101 x 75.5
1998
Courtesy of the Collection of the Singh Twins

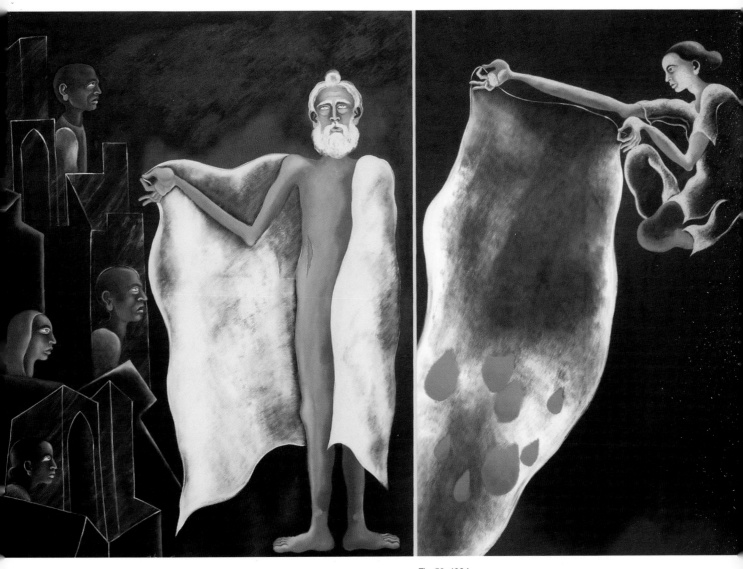

Fig. 59. *1984*
Arpana Caur (b. 1954)
Oil diptych on canvas, 141 x 177.8
2000
Courtesy of the Kapany Collection of
Sikh Art

CONTEMPORARY SIKH ART

Within the exhibition *Sikhs: Legacy of the Punjab,* there are areas for artworks that need to be rotated due to their fragility, or to provide opportunities for the exploration of particular themes. At the exhibition's first opening (at the National Museum of Natural History in July 2004), these areas were dedicated to contemporary Sikh art, including paintings by self-taught artist Arpana Caur, and by twins Amrit and Rabindra Kaur Singh (the "Singh Twins"). The latter paintings fuse an Indian miniature style with contemporary subject-matter (see Mcleod 1991; Randhawa 2000). As a brief introduction to contemporary Sikh art, this chapter describes these Sikh artists and their works, as well as *phulkari*, an additional art form featured in the exhibition. Phulkari are traditional Punjabi textiles that continue to be produced and remain a significant aspect of contemporary Sikh culture.

◄ Fig. 60. *Nyrmla's Wedding II*
The Singh Twins (b. 1966)
Gouache and gold dust on mount board,
76.2 x 50.8
1996
Courtesy of the Collection of the
Singh Twins

The Singh Twins

London-born twins Amrit and Rabindra Kaur Singh work collaboratively on paintings that fuse traditional Indian miniature style with contemporary subjects like Sikh weddings in 20th-century Britain. As Deborah Swallow explains, "the Twins have succeeded in transforming the 'traditional' miniature into an artistic medium which allows them to explore the circumstances of their lives as Asians living in a predominantly western environment" (1999: 16). The twins work in shifts, juxtaposing highly detailed decorative finishes with lively commentary on ethnic, social, and political issues.

Displayed at the opening of the exhibition at the National Museum of Natural History were: "All That I Am" (a portrait and narrative of the Twins' father), "Nyrmla's Wedding II" (on their sisters' wedding), and "1984 (The Storming of the "Golden Temple")."

Fig. 62. *All That I Am* ▶
The Singh Twins (b. 1966)
Gouache and gold dust on mount board, 64 x 45.1
1993-4
Courtesy of the Collection of the Singh Twins

Fig. 61. Rabindra Kaur Singh (left) and Amrit Kaur Singh

Arpana Caur

The works of Indian painter Arpana Caur have been shown around the world. Through symbolic figures and motifs, Caur creates powerful comments on Indian issues. Born in 1954, this self-taught artist paints in a modern, Western style.

In discussing her work, Arpana Caur explains why she is motivated to express herself through traditional Indian motifs: "We have a centuries old tradition that we should acknowledge, and not get lost in the limbo of say American or European art. It's very engulfing, you know. But to incorporate that (tradition) in your own way and therefore pay homage to it by incorporating it. So that it's not lost, it's alive, and it's running in your veins also" (Caur 2011: 13).

Fig. 63. *Sacred Thread*
Arpana Caur (b. 1954)
Oil on canvas, 177.8 x 143.5
2002
Courtesy of the Collection of Sharad and Mahinder Tak

The scissors and thread depicted in this painting refer to a famous account in which Guru Nanak refuses to wear a thread traditionally given to male Hindu children as a marker of the three highest Hindu castes. The map in the background refers to Guru Nanak's extensive travels.

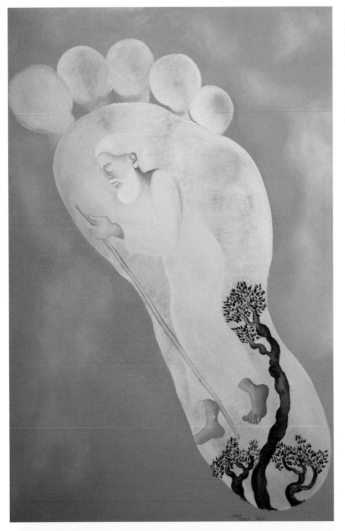

Fig. 64. *Endless Journeys*
Arpana Caur (b. 1954)
Oil on canvas, 174 x 113
2002
Courtesy of the Kapany Collection of
Sikh Art

Arpana Caur expresses her devotion to
Sikhism through her art. In this work,
she depicts Guru Nanak inside a large
footprint because she feels he "spread
his message of love and peace wherever
his feet would take him" (interview, 2004).

Fig. 65. Arpana Caur
Courtesy of the Artist

Phulkari: A Punjabi Textile Art

Phulkari is a Punjabi word meaning "flowered work." For generations, these elaborately hand-embroidered cloths have been part of a Punjabi family's wealth. They were traditionally embroidered by the mother and given to her daughter. The phulkari is often worn by the bride at a special ceremony the day before the wedding, but the cloths also can be hung decoratively or used as a bedspread. Today, clothing and accessories are sometimes made from phulkaris.

Most phulkari textiles feature a basic darning stitch using silk floss. The precise geometric shapes are achieved by counting threads from the underside of the cloth. Characteristically, the vibrant colors—magenta, white, orange, and yellow—are sewn on dyed cotton cloth. In some phulkaris, the colors represent crops and the design a stylized, landscape plan. A fully embroidered work, called a *bagh*, meaning "garden," may take a year or more to complete.

Fig. 66. Phulkari (*Chadder* style)
Cotton and silk floss
c. 1940
Courtesy of the Collection of Mrs. Marian Chandu Ray Bhukari

The orange, white, and pink half-circles represent cherry trees in the autumn. This phulkari is one of a series that depicts fruit trees during the seasons.

Fig. 67. Phulkari (*Bagh* style)
Cotton and silk floss
Middle 20th century
Courtesy of Mrs. Kulkreet K. Chaudhary

This family heirloom was brought from
India and passed down from mother to
daughter, as is the Punjabi custom.

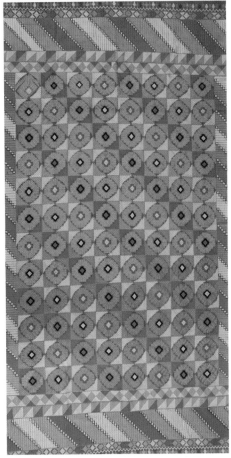

Fig. 68. Phulkari (Eastern Punjab)
Cotton and silk floss
c. 1900
Courtesy of Dr. Sohan S. and Mrs. Kamal
K. Chaudhry

9

SIKH MUSIC: SOUNDS OF FAITH AND CELEBRATION

Sikh Sacred Music

Because Guru Nanak believed music inspired the mind, music has always been an integral part of Sikh devotion. Each *shabad,* or scriptural composition, contains a special message. The musicians sing the words to an Indian *rāg,* a musical form that describes a particular mood. From 31 classical rāgs, Sikh musicians select one that is appropriate for the time of day and season (see Singh, Khushwant 2008).

◄ Fig. 69. *Dhol* drummer Lal Singh Bhatti at the opening of the exhibition *Sikhs: Legacy of the Punjab* at the National Museum of Natural History, Smithsonian Institution. (July 24, 2004)

Traditionally, men play the *dhol* drum. It hangs from a strap and both ends are beaten with the hands or with sticks. One drumhead is coated inside to produce a deeper sound.

The *tabla,* or *jori,* accompanies the singers and harmonium. Played with the fingers of the right hand, the small wooden drum with a dark center produces light tapping sounds. The larger, metal drum makes lower, more powerful beats.

Fig. 70. Sikh *rāgis,* or musicians, sit on the floor to play beside the Guru Granth Sahib. Since the turn of the 20th century, the traditional instruments to accompany the service have been the harmonium and tabla. (May 2004)

Fig. 71. Tabla Drums *(Jori)*
Wood, metal, skin, and rope
20th century

Fig. 72. Harmonium
Wood, metal, and other materials
20th century

Introduced by Portuguese missionaries in
the 1800s, this hand-pumped reed organ
has replaced most stringed instruments
in the Sikh service. One hand plays the
keys while the other operates the bellows.
Generally, the traditional service includes
two harmoniums.

Fig. 73. *Raja Dhian Singh Entertained by Musicians*
Artist Unknown
Gouache on paper
c. 1830-40
Courtesy of the Kapany Collection of Sikh Art

This painting shows the lifestyle enjoyed by the Punjabi ruling class in the early 19th century. Seated in a jeweled European-style chair with formal Mughal-style gardens and fountain in the background, and wearing the latest Arab-influenced turban, Raja Dhian Singh is fanned under a canopy while musicians entertain him. Dhian Singh was the prime minister under Ranjit Singh.

Musical Heritage of the Punjab

Drawing on many South Asian traditions, contemporary Punjabi music enhances all Sikh holidays and celebrations. The percolating rhythms of the *dhol* drum are increasingly heard outside the Punjab, as part of the world music movement and also in Western popular music (see Pande 1999; Singh, Gurmukh 2003). The exhibition *Sikhs: Legacy of the Punjab* includes a graphic musical display panel that allows visitors to learn more about Sikh music and listen to audio samples. The display panel features three varieties of music that play different roles in Sikh celebrations, worship, and cultural life: *jago, dhadi,* and *bhangra.*

Fig. 74. A young visitor to the National Museum of Natural History explores Sikh music through a graphic music display panel.

Jago

The night before a Sikh wedding, the bride's family hosts a gathering called a *jago* where women sing and dance together. One instrument often played at a jago is the *dholki*, a smaller version of the *dhol* drum.

Fig. 75. *Dholki*
Wood, rope, and skin
20th century

Dhadi: Songs of Heroism

A *dhadi* is a minstrel or bard who sings ballads in celebration of Sikh heroes, history, and faith. A *dhadi jatha* is a group of four dhadis and usually includes a *sarangi* player, two *dhadd* players, and a narrator/singer. Dhadi performances often inspire Sikhs by linking present-day challenges to Sikh history and heritage.

Bhangra: Classic Punjab, International Sensation

Bhangra originated as the traditional dance of Punjabi harvest festivals enjoyed by Sikhs and non-Sikhs alike. Although it is not a musical form specific to Sikhism, it emerged out of the Punjabi cultural milieu in which Sikh culture and traditions figure prominently. Today it is known worldwide as a form of popular music that was developed and popularized in Britain during the 1980's by first and second generation Indian immigrants (Roy 2010: 1). With the addition of modern instruments to the infectious rhythms and lively lyrics of bhangra, the appeal of the music has grown tremendously (see Pande 1999).

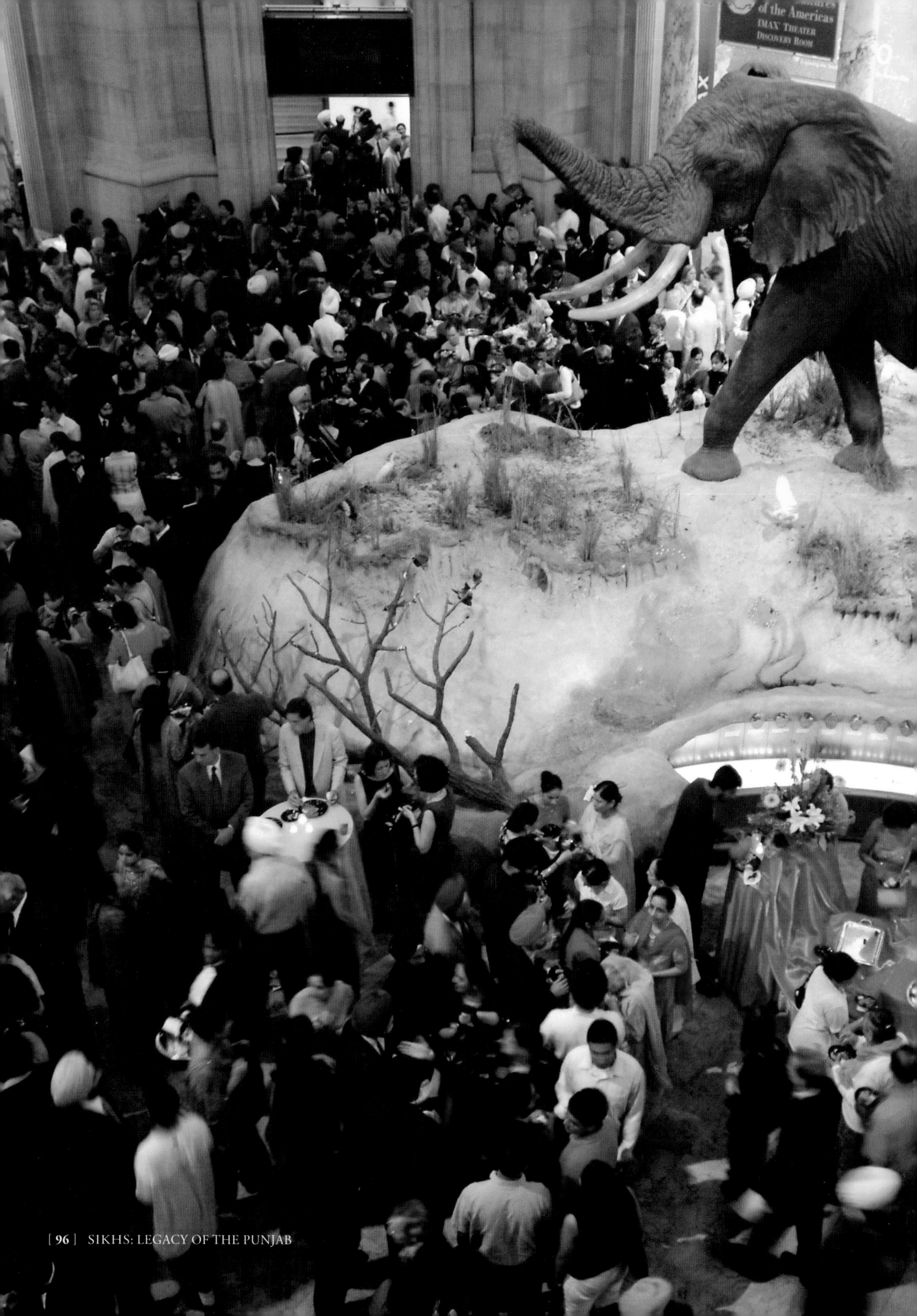
of the Americas
IMAX THEATER
DISCOVERY ROOM

EPILOGUE

The Sikh Heritage Project, as a museum-community partnership which led to the exhibition *Sikhs: Legacy of the Punjab*, has produced many positive outcomes. The exhibition is surely the most visible of them.

The mode in which this exhibition was developed, within a larger framework of community involvement, reflects a changing view of the nature of museum curatorship as a social practice.[2] Such a view places museum exhibitions within a more holistic, integrated, and culturally relative approach to curatorial work that explores and includes the relationships among (museum) objects, people, and society in social and cultural contexts beyond the museum collection or exhibition. Museum-based projects that include exhibitions increasingly involve integrating events that bring together a community or communities to celebrate or re-assert shared values, in addition to the traditional curatorial responsibilities, such as the responsibility to preserve and care for collections, to add new information through research on collections, and to accurately interpret and present objects in exhibitions and other media.

◄ Fig. 76. Reception in celebration of the opening of the *Sikhs: Legacy of the Punjab* exhibition at the Smithsonian's National Museum of Natural History. (July 24, 2004)

[2] See Kreps, Christina (2003). "Curatorship as Social Practice." *Curator: The Museum Journal,* 46(3):311-324 (July 2003). See also Paul Michael Taylor's (2004) "Sikh Heritage at the Smithsonian." *Journal of Punjab Studies,* 11(2):221-236 (Special issue: "Culture of Punjab"). (Cf. Nightingale and Swallow, 2003.)

Nevertheless, the issues of cultural representation arising during a project of this kind do not easily fit conventional frameworks of analysis. For example, if one considers the project through relations among parts of the triad consisting of (1) a museum (collecting/display institution), (2) a people whose culture is the subject of the museum's representation (cultural tradition exhibited), and (3) an expected or targeted audience ("viewership"), one finds considerable overlap. Taylor has elsewhere used this triad to consider the changing ways in which Indonesian material culture has been represented in museums and their predecessors, from the Renaissance to contemporary museums in the Republic of Indonesia.[3]

For the production of *Sikhs: Legacy of the Punjab*, the museum in this case had virtually no Sikh collections, and in the end relied heavily on loaned materials (largely from a few prominent Sikh collectors) while planning to build collections later in this area. In addition, the Smithsonian's "Sikh Heritage Project," which came to include this exhibition among its goals, was from the beginning a team effort in which a growing community of supporters not only provided financial backing for the exhibition, but also helped to organize regular community-building meetings and events that turned the effort into a shared community project.

This Project's intended audience, however, always included a wide American and international public. This broad audience for the discovery of Sikh cultural heritage facilitated two related objectives. First, the exhibition helped a broad public learn about a culture, history, and religion of which they often had little prior acquaintance and understanding. Second, the exhibition provided

---

[3] Taylor (1995) "Collecting Icons of Power and Identity: Transformations of Indonesian Material Culture in the Museum Context." *Cultural Dynamics* 7(1):101-124. (Special issue: "Museums and Changing Perspectives of Culture," ed. by Anthony Shelton.)

an important social space for Sikhs themselves, who could take pride in seeing their traditions among those represented at America's "national museum." Museum staff members found themselves "translating" Sikh self-representations for a wider audience and, like all translators, modifying the content in the process. Sikh meta-narratives of Sikh history became incorporated into the exhibition; but so did other aspects of Sikh "heritage," including everyday secular music and contemporary celebrations. For Sikh-Americans participating in the process, this led to a transformation or expansion of the range of objects thought to represent Sikh "heritage" – as it became clear that even family albums, mementos, and everyday household objects might be included.

The Sikh Heritage Project, and the exhibition *Sikhs: Legacy of the Punjab*, attempted to seek and to integrate community involvement in ways well beyond the norm in contemporary museum work. In fact, an active group of community members was involved even in the early decision of whether to focus our collective effort toward exhibition or toward other potential goals of the Project. This project successfully encompassed many examples of co-curatorship with a large community that arrived at and presented decisions in a process which proved to be quite effective. The authors are grateful that, among those community members, many suggested recording key aspects of the exhibition within this book, whose text has benefitted from their many suggestions and whose production and printing has also been made possible by their continuing support and encouragement.

Paul Michael Taylor
Robert Pontsioen
Washington, D.C., USA – July 2014

BIBLIOGRAPHY AND SUGGESTED READINGS

Alag, Sarup Singh. 2005. *Mistaken Identity of the Sikhs.* 15th revised deluxe edition. Ludhiana, India: Alag Shabad Yug Charitable Trust.

Avtar Singh.1970. *Ethics of the Sikhs.* Patalia: Punjabi University.

Bharadia, Seema. 1966. *The Arts of the Sikh Kingdoms: The Canadian Collections.* Toronto: Royal Ontario Museum.

Brown, Kerry. 1999. *Sikh Art and Literature.* New York: Routledge.

Caur, Arpana (ed.) 2011. *Arpana Caur: Abstract Figurations.* New Delhi: Academy of Fine Arts and Literature (India)

Caur, Arpana, Suneet Chopra and D.J. Singh. 2001. *The Art of Arpana Caur.* (Pocket Art Series). New Delhi: Lustre Press.

Caur, Arpana, and Ernst W. Koelnsperger. 2008. *Arpana Caur: The Passion with Time.* New Delhi: Academy of Fine Arts and Literature.

Cheema, Iqtidar Karamat. 2010. *The Third Apostle: Life and Contributions of Guru Amar Das.* Waremme, Belgium: Sikh University Press.

Cole, W. Owen, and Piara Singh Sambhi. 1978. *The Sikhs: Their Religious Beliefs and Practices.* London; Boston: Routledge & K. Paul.

Dhillon, Gurdarshan Singh. 1999. *Khalsa: Its Role and Relevance.* New Delhi, India: Gurdwara Sikh Management Committee.

Duggal, Devinder Singh. 2006. *The Truth about the Sikhs.* Amristar: Dharam Parchar Committee / Shiromani Gurdwara Parbandhak Committee.

Duggal, Kartar Singh. 2005. *Sikh Gurus: Their Lives and Teachings.* New Delhi, India: UBSPD.

Gill, Pritam Singh. 1975. *Heritage of Sikh Culture: Society, Morality, Art.* Jullundur: New Academic Pub. Co.

Goswamy, B.N. 2000. *Piety and Splendour: Sikh Heritage in Art.* New Delhi: National Museum.

Grewal, J.S. 2009. *The Sikhs: Ideology, Institutions, and Identity.* New Delhi: Oxford University Press.

Herrli, Hans. 2004. *The Coins of the Sikhs.* 2nd revised and augmented edition. New Delhi: Munshiram Manoharlal Publishers.

Hocking, Bree. 2004. "Natural History Museum Opens New Exhibit on Sikhs." *Roll Call,* July 22, 2004.

India Journal. 2004. "Smithsonian Museum Opens Sikh Heritage Gallery" (by "A Staff Reporter"). *India Journal* 16 (7): 1, 16, 18, 20.

Jaspal Singh. 2010. *Guru Granth Sahib: The Sikh Scripture*. New Delhi: K.K. Publications.

Jodhka, Surinder S. 2010. *The Sikhs Today: A Development Profile*. New Delhi: Indian Institute of Dalit Studies.

Kang, Kanwarjit Singh. 1988. *Punjab: Art and Culture*. Delhi: Atma Ram & Sons.

Kaur, Arunjeet. 2010. *The Sikhs in Singapore*. Singapore: Institute of Southeast Asian Studies.

Kaur Singh, Amrit and Rabindra Kaur Singh. 1999. *Bindhu's Wedding*. Palo Alta, CA: Sikh Foundation in Association with Chardikalaa Sikh Community Center.

—1999. *TwinPerspectives: Paintings by Amrit and Rabindra KD Kaur Singh*. United Kingdom: Twin Studios.

—2005. *Worlds A-part: Paintings by the Singh Twins*. United Kingdom: Twin Studios.

Kaur, Surjeet. 2003. *Amongst the Sikhs: Reaching for the Stars*. New Delhi: Lotus Collection.

Kreps, Christina. 2003. "Curatorship as Social Practice." *Curator: The Museum Journal*, 46(3):311-324 (July 2003).

Madra, Amandeep Singh, Parmjit Singh, and Sikh Foundation. 1999. *Warrior Saints: Three Centuries of the Sikh Military Tradition*. London, New York: I.B. Taurus in association with the Sikh Foundation.

Mann, Gurinder Singh. 2001. *The Making of Sikh Scripture*. Oxford; New York: Oxford University Press.

—2004. *Sikhism*. Upper Saddle River, NJ: Prentice Hall.

Manukhani, Gobind Singh. 2004. *Introduction to Sikhism: 125 Basic Questions and Answers on Sikh Religion and History*. New Delhi: Hemkunt Press.

Massey, James. 2010. *A Contemporary Look at Sikh Religion: Essays on Scripture, Identity, Creation, Spirituality, Charity and Interfaith Dialogue*. New Delhi: Manohar Publishers & Distributors.

Mcleod, W.H. 1991. *Popular Sikh Art*. Delhi; New York: Oxford University Press.

—1991. *Discovering the Sikhs: Autobiography of a Historian*. Delhi; Columbia, MO: Permanent Block.

—2002. *Historical Dictionary of Sikhism*. New Delhi; New York: Oxford University Press.

Mitta, Manoj and Harvinder Singh Phoolka. 2008. *When a Tree Shook Delhi: The 1984 Carnage and its Aftermath*. New Delhi: Lotus Collection, an imprint of Roli Books.

Nesbitt, Eleanor M. and Gopinder Kaur. 1999. *Guru Nanak*. Calgary: Bayeaux.

Nightingale, Eithne and Deborah Swallow. 2003. "The Arts of the Sikh Kingdoms: Collaborating with a Community." In: Alison K. Brown and Laura Peers (eds.), *Museums and Source Communities: A Routledge Reader*. New York: Routledge.

Oberoi, Harjot. 1994. *The Construction of Religious Boundaries: Culture, Identity and Diversity in the Sikh Tradition*. Delhi: Oxford University Press.

Pande, Alka. 1999. *From Mustard Fields to Disco Lights: Folk Music & Musical Instruments of Punjab*. Ahmedabad: Mapin Publishing.

Randhawa, T.S. 2000. *The Sikhs: Images of a Heritage*. New Delhi: Prakash Books.

Roy, Anjali Gera. 2010. *Bhangra Moves: From Ludhiana to London and Beyond*. Burlington, VT: Ashgate Press.

Seetal, Sohan Singh. 1970. *How Fell the Sikh Kingdom?* Ludhiana: Lyall Book Depot.

Shaw-Eagle, Joanna. 2004. "Art from the Punjab." *The Washington Times*, Saturday, August 7.

Sidhu, Amarpal. 2010. *The First Anglo-Sikh War*. Stroud: Amberly.

Sikka, Ajit Singh. 1973. *Beacons of Light*. Ludhiana: Bee Kay Publications.

Singh, Avtar. 1970. *Ethics of the Sikhs*. Patiala: Punjabi University.

Singh, Bhai Sahib Sirdar Kapur. 2002. *Sikhism and the World Society*. Amristar: Dharam Parchar Committee / Shiromani Gurdwara Parbandhak Committee.

Singh, Dalip. 1999. *Sikhism: In the Words of the Guru*. Amristar: Lok Sahit Prakashan.

Singh, Gopal. 1988. *A History of the Sikh People, 1469 – 1988*. 2nd revised and updated edition. New Delhi: Allied Publishers.

Singh, Gurbachan. 1998. *The Sikhs: Faith, Philosophy & Folk*. New Delhi: Lustre Press, Pvt. Ltd.

Singh, Gurbakhsh. 2005. *The Sikh Faith: A Universal Message*. Armistar: Singh Bros.

Singh, Gurmukh. 2003. *The Global Indian: The Rise of Sikhs Abroad*. New Delhi: Rupa & Co.

Singh, Harbans. 1999. *The Heritage of the Sikhs*. 3rd Edition. New Delhi: Manohar.

Singh, I.J. 2001. *The Sikh Way: A Pilgrim's Progress*. Guelph, Ontario: Centennial Foundation.

Singh, Jasprit and Teresa Singh. 1998. *Style of the Lion: The Sikhs*. Ann Arbor, Michigan: Akal Publications.

Singh, K.P. 2003. *The Art and Spirit of K.P. Singh*. Indianapolis: Guild Press-Emmis Publishing.

Singh, Khushwant. 2004. *A History of the Sikhs*. (2 v.) 2nd edition. New Delhi: Oxford University Press.

—2008. *Songs of the Gurus: From Nanak to Gobind Singh*. New Delhi: Viking Ravi Dayal Publisher.

Singh, Meji. 2004. *A Sikh's Paradigm for Universal Peace*. Walnut Creek, CA: Pavior Publishing.

Singh, Mike. 2004. "*Sikhs: Legacy of the Punjab* Exhibition at the Smithsonian." *India Post*, September 8.

Singh, Nikky-Gurinder Kaur. 2001. *The Name of my Beloved: Verses of the Sikh Gurus*. New Delhi: Penguin Books India.

Singh, Pashaura. 2003. *The Bhagats of the Guru Granth Sahib: Sikh Self-definition and the Bhagat Bani*. New Delhi: Oxford University Press.

Singh, Pashaura and Louise E. Fenech (eds.) 2014. *The Oxford Handbook of Sikh Studies*. Oxford: Oxford University Press.

Singh, Patwant and Gurmeet Thukral. 1992. *Gudwaras in India and Around the World*. New Delhi: Himalayan Books.

Singh, Preetam. 2000. *Baisakhi of the Khalsa Panth*. New Delhi: Sanbun Publishers.

Singh, Puran: 1998. *The Book of Ten Masters*. Amristar: Singh Bros.

Singh, S. Kulmohan. 1994. *Shahadat Naama: Brief Account of Sikh Martyrs*. New Delhi: Delhi Sikh Gurdwara Management Committee.

Singh, Sardar Kapur. 2000. *Impact of Sikhism on Modern India*. New Delhi: Delhi Sikh Gurdwara Management Committee.

Singh, Sikandar and Roopinder Singh. 2012. *Sikh Heritage: Ethos and Relics*. New Delhi: Rupa Publications India.

Singh, Teja. 1990. *The Sikh Religion: An Outline of its Doctrines*. New Delhi: Delhi Sikh Gurdwara Management Committee.

Swallow, Deborah. 1999. "…To a Modern Revival." In: Amrit Kaur Singh and Rabindra Kaur Singh, *TwinPerspectives: Paintings by Amrit and Rabindra KD Kaur Singh*. United Kingdom: Twin Studios.

Taylor, Paul Michael. 1995. "Collecting Icons of Power and Identity: Transformations of Indonesian Material Culture in the Museum Context." *Cultural Dynamics* 7(1):101-124. (Special issue: "Museums and Changing Perspectives of Culture," ed. by Anthony Shelton.)

—2004. "Sikh Heritage at the Smithsonian." *Journal of Punjab Studies* 11(2): 221-236. (Special issue: "Culture of Punjab.")

—2012. "Introduction: Perspectives on the Punjab's Most Meaningful Heirlooms." In: Sikandar Singh and Roopinder Singh, *Sikh Heritage: Ethos and Relics*. New Delhi: Rupa.

Taylor, Paul Michael and Christopher Lotis. 2008. *Flagship of a Fleet: A Korea Gallery Guide*. Washington, D.C.: Asian Cultural History Program, Smithsonian Institution.

Voices across Boundaries. 2004. "Photoessay of an Exhibition: Sikhs, a Punjab Legacy". *Voices across Boundaries* (Fall), pp. 53-56.

Yeager, Tami R. (Director). 2007. *A Dream in Doubt*. (Motion Picture. Length: 56 minutes.) TRY Productions and Independent Television Service (ITVS), in association with Center for Asian American Media (CAAM). [Republished in DVD format, 2008, San Francisco, CA: Center for Asian American Media.]

PHOTO CREDITS

Smithsonian Institution, Asian Cultural History Program: figures 3, 5, 9, 10, 11, 18, 33, 43, 54, 57, 72, 73, 74, 75, 77, back cover middle

Smithsonian Institution, Chip Clark: front cover left, figures 1, 6, 14, 15, 22, 23, 25, 27, 29, 45, 46, 47, 70, back cover main, back cover top

Smithsonian Institution, Neil Greentree: figure 26

Smithsonian Institution, John Steiner: figures 8, 39

Howard Barlow: figure 61

Arpana Caur: figures 59, 65

Bruno Frohlich: front cover main, figures 4, 41, 42, 48, 51, 78

Kapany Collection of Sikh Art: figure 73

Michel Lee: figures 13, 32, 56, 69, 76

Robert Pontsioen: figure 71

William Bradford Smith: figure 63

Hanna Szczepanowska: figures 12, 28, 30, 35, 36, 37, 38, 44, 66, 67

The Singh Twins: figures 58, 60, 62

Jasper Waugh-Quasebarth: front cover middle, front cover right, figures 2, 7, 17, 19, 20, 21, 24, 31, 34, 49, 50, 52, 53, 55, 64, 68, back cover bottom

Endpaper: Monochrome traced outline of central panel patterns from Phulkari shown in Fig. 68

Fig. 77. Stone mosaic at the Darbar ▶ Sahib, Amritsar, Punjab, India (June 2006)

Fig. 78. Gurdwara Takht Sri Kesgarh Sahib in Anandpur Sahib, Punjab, India. (2006)